Online Privacy 101

Simple Steps to Protect Your Identity, Devices, and Personal Data Online

By Joe Correa

Published by Live Stronger Faster

This book is for educational and informational purposes only. The author and publisher are not engaged in rendering legal, financial, or other professional advice. Readers should consult a qualified professional before making any financial decisions.

First Edition

Table of Contents

Introduction

In a world increasingly driven by data, the concept of online privacy has become more than a preference—it's a necessity. Every click, swipe, and voice command you make is part of a growing digital profile used to target you, sell to you, manipulate you, or even steal from you. Yet for most people, online privacy remains a vague idea, often dismissed as something for "hackers and tech nerds" or conspiracy theorists. The reality is far more personal—and far more urgent.

Online privacy isn't just about avoiding ads. It's about protecting your identity, your money, your family, your career, and your future. The data being collected about you—often without your full understanding—is used to influence your decisions, monitor your behavior, and in some cases, control outcomes in your life. Whether it's a breached password, a leaked credit card number, or location data being tracked and sold, the consequences of neglecting online privacy are very real and very expensive.

The good news is: you don't need to be a cybersecurity expert to protect yourself. With a few key tools, simple habits, and a better understanding of how your data is collected, you can take back control. This book is your step-by-step guide to doing just that.

You'll learn how to:

- Identify and eliminate the biggest privacy risks in your daily routine
- Strengthen your passwords and authentication
- Use private browsers and VPNs to shield your internet activity
- Understand how apps, social media, and search engines collect your data
- Prevent identity theft, phishing, and financial fraud
- Set up private communication tools for texting and email
- Protect your children and family from online exposure

Each chapter offers simple, actionable solutions based on what real people can do today. We'll cut through the jargon, debunk common myths, and focus on what truly works for the average user—whether you're on a smartphone, laptop, tablet, or smart TV.

This book is part of the larger *Cyber Shield Academy* series, but it's designed to be complete on its own. If you're new to cybersecurity, you're in the right place. If you're not sure where to start, you'll find a clear roadmap here. And if you've already taken some privacy steps but want to go further, we'll cover more advanced strategies too.

Why does this matter now? Because the privacy landscape is changing faster than ever. Laws are evolving, surveillance is increasing, and tech companies are finding new ways to track your behavior. From smart home devices to AI voice assistants to facial recognition in stores, your privacy is being challenged in ways most people don't even realize.

We are living through the biggest shift in personal security since the rise of the internet. Just as seatbelts became standard in cars once people understood the risks of driving, online privacy tools and habits must become standard in our digital lives. The earlier you start, the safer you'll be.

This book is not about hiding from the world. It's about navigating it with intelligence. It's about choosing what to share, when to share it, and with whom—on your terms, not theirs.

So let's begin your privacy upgrade. Turn the page, hit play, and get ready to take back your power in the digital age. This is your blueprint for safer browsing, stronger habits, and total peace of mind online.

Chapter 1: Why Online Privacy Matters More Than Ever

We live in a time when data is more valuable than oil. That's not a metaphor—it's an economic truth. Every major tech company today is a data company at its core. From Google to Meta, Amazon to TikTok, your personal information is being collected, analyzed, packaged, and sold in real time. And while you may not feel the impact of this data trade every day, it affects everything from the ads you see to the prices you pay, the jobs you qualify for, and even the news you're exposed to.

But why should you care about online privacy? Isn't this just the cost of convenience in a digital world? After all, we've gotten used to using "free" apps in exchange for giving away our data. That's the deal, right?

The problem is, that "free" deal is much more expensive than most people realize. The data you give away is being used to:

- Build detailed behavioral profiles on you
- Influence your political opinions
- Control what content you see and don't see
- Predict your future behavior and purchases

- Sell your information to third parties without your full consent

This level of surveillance was once the realm of spy movies. Today, it's part of your everyday life. Your smartphone is tracking your location. Your social media profiles are scanning your facial expressions. Your browser history is being stored and sold. Even your email and messages can be analyzed by algorithms to predict your moods and habits.

It's not just advertisers who want your data. Cybercriminals want it, too. With the right bits of information—like your email address, date of birth, or mother's maiden name—they can open credit cards in your name, drain your bank accounts, or impersonate you to others. Identity theft is no longer rare. It's a global epidemic.

And then there's the psychological cost. Studies show that constant digital surveillance makes people more anxious, less creative, and more likely to self-censor. When you know you're being watched, you act differently. Online privacy isn't just about protecting your data—it's about protecting your freedom to think, speak, and explore without fear.

So what's the solution? It starts with awareness. You don't need to disconnect from the internet or live off the grid. You simply need to be intentional about how you interact online. This includes:

- Reading app permissions before installing
- Using privacy-focused browsers and search engines
- Updating your privacy settings on all social platforms
- Avoiding free Wi-Fi networks that aren't secure
- Using password managers and two-factor authentication
- Encrypting your messages and emails
- Thinking twice before sharing sensitive information online

None of these steps are extreme. They're simple, realistic, and incredibly effective once they become part of your digital routine.

The bottom line is this: online privacy isn't about hiding. It's about having control. Control over your data. Control over your time. Control over your identity and your future. And in a world where everything is being tracked, control is the new luxury.

In the following chapters, we'll explore every layer of your digital life and show you how to protect it—clearly, practically, and step-by-step.

Now, let's bring this lesson to life with a true-to-life story...

It all started with a forgotten password reset. Maria, a 38-year-old graphic designer living in Atlanta, had just wrapped up a busy morning of client work when she got an email that stopped her cold. The subject line read: "Your Apple ID has been locked due to suspicious activity." Her heart jumped. She hadn't logged in that morning, and she wasn't using her Apple account on any new device.

Thinking it might be spam, she clicked on the sender details. It looked legitimate. The logo, the language, even the return address mimicked Apple's perfectly. Without thinking twice, she clicked the link, entered her credentials, and hit submit.

What happened next unraveled her digital life.

Within hours, she was logged out of all her Apple devices. Her phone stopped receiving texts. Her MacBook was locked remotely. And worst of all—her bank had flagged two large unauthorized transactions from Apple Pay. She was locked out of her email, her PayPal, and her social media. It was like her identity had vanished into someone else's hands.

In a panic, Maria called Apple Support. The voice on the other end confirmed her fears: she'd been phished. The email wasn't real. She had given away her Apple ID and password to a cybercriminal—who immediately used it to reset everything linked to that account. Her photos. Her notes. Her contacts. Her entire digital life.

The recovery process was slow and painful. She had to verify her identity with multiple banks, report the theft to the police, call credit bureaus, and explain to clients why she'd missed meetings and lost files. The emotional toll was even heavier than the financial one. She felt violated, ashamed, and deeply anxious. "I didn't think something like this could happen to me," she told a friend. "I thought I was careful."

Maria wasn't careless—she was uninformed. Like millions of people, she had never heard of phishing emails. She used the same password across multiple platforms. She didn't use two-factor authentication. And she had no idea her actions were being tracked online daily.

It wasn't until after this digital disaster that Maria started learning. She began using a password manager. She installed a VPN. She encrypted her devices. She turned on two-factor authentication for everything. And slowly, she began to rebuild.

Her story isn't unique. It's a warning—and a wake-up call. Privacy breaches don't always look like masked hackers in hoodies. They look like normal people clicking on the wrong link or trusting the wrong app. They happen in everyday moments—when you're distracted, busy, or just trying to get something done quickly.

But there's power in awareness. Maria turned her mistake into motivation. Today, she teaches other freelancers how to stay safe online. She shares her experience openly, hoping others won't have to learn the hard way.

The lesson? Online privacy matters. Not tomorrow. Not next month. Now.

Chapter 2: The Digital Trail You Leave Behind

Every time you go online—whether to shop, scroll, read the news, or check the weather—you're leaving behind a digital trail. This trail is a collection of data points that silently reveal who you are, what you think, where you've been, and what you're likely to do next. Most people don't realize how detailed this trail is or how many entities are watching and recording it. Your clicks, swipes, search terms, locations, purchases, video views, app usage, and even how fast you scroll—all of it contributes to your digital footprint. And most of this happens in the background, without your active awareness or consent.

The concept of cookies is one of the first breadcrumbs in your online trail. Originally designed to improve user experience—like remembering what's in your shopping cart or keeping you logged in—cookies have evolved. Today, third-party cookies are one of the primary tools advertisers use to follow you across websites, collecting data to build a behavioral profile. These profiles are then used for hyper-targeted advertising. Ever searched for something on Google and then seen ads for it on Facebook or Instagram? That's your digital trail in action.

But cookies are only the beginning. Websites and mobile apps use trackers, beacons, pixels, and device fingerprinting to monitor what you do—even if you're not logged in. For example, your phone might send your location data to dozens of companies via apps that don't even need GPS permissions. They track through Bluetooth signals, Wi-Fi networks, and IP address triangulation. Your weather app, flashlight app, or mobile game may seem harmless, but many are quietly harvesting your location, contacts, and browsing behavior.

Metadata—the information about your activity—is another overlooked component. It's not what you said in a message, but who you sent it to, at what time, for how long, and from what device. Metadata is incredibly revealing. It can map your relationships, routines, moods, and habits. Governments and private companies alike analyze this kind of data to predict behavior or flag certain patterns.

Even your search engine history contributes to your digital trail. Google alone keeps logs of what you search, when you search it, which results you click, how long you stay, and which device you used. This data paints a picture of your interests, fears, goals, and even your health or financial situation. And unless you've changed your settings, much of this information is retained indefinitely.

Social media adds another powerful layer. What you post, like, comment on, or even hover over is recorded. Algorithms study your engagement to prioritize your feed—but also to refine your psychological profile. Platforms know your political leanings, religious beliefs, relationship status, income range, and more—sometimes even more accurately than your closest friends. And even if you're not on social media, others can tag you in photos or posts, creating what's called a "shadow profile" built from data others have provided.

The devices you use, the browsers you prefer, and the Wi-Fi networks you connect to also leave identifiable traces. This is called device fingerprinting. It involves collecting information about your screen resolution, browser version, fonts installed, time zone, and plugins. This combination is often unique to you, making it possible to track you even if you clear your cookies or use incognito mode.

The risks of leaving a large, unmanaged digital trail are serious. For one, it makes you an easier target for identity theft, scams, and phishing. Criminals don't need your Social Security number to impersonate you—they can use publicly available information to guess passwords, answer security questions, or send personalized scam emails that trick you into giving up sensitive data. Your data trail can also be sold and resold by data brokers, who collect it from various sources, package it into profiles, and sell it to advertisers, insurance companies, credit bureaus, and more.

And let's not forget the psychological effects. When people realize they're being watched, they often begin to self-censor. This is called the "chilling effect," where individuals stop searching for certain topics, expressing opinions, or exploring ideas simply because they fear being judged or monitored. This loss of freedom is subtle but damaging—it erodes creativity, curiosity, and authenticity.

Fortunately, there are steps you can take to reduce your digital trail. Start by using private or incognito browsing modes, though be aware these are limited—they don't hide your IP or prevent tracking by websites. Switch to privacy-focused browsers like Brave or Firefox and use search engines like DuckDuckGo that don't track your queries. Install tracker-blocking extensions like uBlock Origin, Privacy Badger, or Ghostery. Use a VPN to hide your IP address and encrypt your internet traffic, especially when using public Wi-Fi.

Review the permissions on all your apps. Ask yourself: does this calculator app really need access to my camera? Revoke permissions that aren't essential. Delete old apps you no longer use, and be wary of free apps that monetize your data.

On your smartphone, turn off location services for all but the apps that truly need it—like maps or ride-sharing services.

Finally, take control of your online accounts. Regularly clear your browsing history and cookies. Log out of accounts when not in use. Adjust your privacy settings on social platforms to limit who can see your posts and data. And sign up for data breach monitoring tools like HaveIBeenPwned.com to check if your email or passwords have been compromised.

Your digital trail is powerful—but it can be managed. Like footprints in the sand, it doesn't have to last forever. With the right tools and habits, you can reduce your visibility, protect your identity, and take back control of your online presence.

Who is Jordan?

Jordan was the kind of guy who loved technology. He had the newest phone every year, synced every smart home device, and rarely left a store without scanning a QR code or downloading a rewards app. His life was seamless—connected, convenient, and fast. But he never gave a second thought to what happened in the background. That was until a job interview changed everything.

He'd applied for a digital marketing position with a mid-sized software company. His resume was solid, his experience strong. The recruiter loved him. "You're a great fit," she said on the phone. "We'll just do one last round of screening with our risk and compliance team."

A week passed. Then another. Jordan followed up twice. Finally, he got an email: "We've decided to move forward with other candidates. Thank you for your interest." No explanation. No feedback.

Confused, Jordan messaged the recruiter on LinkedIn. She hesitated but eventually responded: "Off the record... it looks like something in your online data flagged you as high risk. I don't have details, but their AI systems use public data, social media, and web activity to create risk profiles. I'm sorry."

His stomach dropped. What "online data"? He wasn't a criminal. He didn't post offensive content. He was just... online.

Jordan started digging. He Googled himself. His LinkedIn and Instagram were fine—mostly travel photos and work stuff. But then he found a people-search site that listed his full name, age, past addresses, and even his old phone numbers. Clicking deeper, it showed his relatives, political donations, traffic tickets, even his old blog posts from college that he had long forgotten. It felt like a digital dossier—a file he never consented to, never knew existed.

Then came the ads. He realized he was being targeted constantly. He searched for health insurance once and got bombarded with spam calls for weeks. He liked one article about cryptocurrency on Facebook and started getting pushed into fringe financial groups. His YouTube recommendations had taken a weird turn too—he couldn't even remember watching half the things now showing up.

The more he looked, the more he realized: he was being watched. All the time.

He installed a browser extension called Ghostery. Within seconds, it showed that one website had over 40 trackers—some he'd never heard of. He tried switching to incognito mode. That helped a little. Then he downloaded Brave, a browser that blocked ads and trackers by default. It felt different—quieter. Less invasive.

He checked the settings on his apps. His flashlight app had access to his microphone. His weather app was collecting location data 24/7. His notes app had permission to access his contacts. He began revoking permissions, uninstalling apps, and turning off location services for everything but essentials. His phone suddenly seemed a lot more private.

Still shaken, he went deeper. He looked into how companies use "device fingerprinting" to track users even without cookies.

How metadata from his emails and messages could be used to map his relationships. How data brokers harvested information from public sources, store purchases, and even smart home devices to build and sell profiles like his to advertisers, insurers, and employers.

Jordan had always believed, “If I have nothing to hide, I have nothing to fear.” But now, he realized that wasn't the point. The point was control. Or rather, the lack of it. His entire digital life had been monitored, recorded, and repackaged—without his permission and with real-world consequences.

He felt violated.

But Jordan wasn’t one to stay powerless. He turned it into a mission. He signed up for privacy alerts to monitor his data. He used a VPN. He started using an encrypted email service. He deleted old social media accounts he no longer used. He even wrote to data broker sites requesting to opt out and have his profile removed.

He began advising his friends and coworkers too. “Just because something’s free doesn’t mean it’s safe,” he’d say. “Your data is the product.” They listened—some skeptically, some with genuine concern. But they couldn’t deny the results when Jordan showed them screenshots of how many trackers he'd blocked in a single day.

One friend asked, "So what—are you going off the grid now?" Jordan smiled. "No. I'm just not leaving the door wide open anymore."

A few months later, he reapplied for a job—this time with a startup that valued privacy and ethics. During the interview, he shared what he'd learned, how he protected himself, and how it impacted his view on marketing and digital behavior. The interviewer was impressed. "We need more people who actually understand the risks behind the data," she said.

Jordan got the job.

His story is a reminder that our digital footprints are more powerful than we realize. They can shape opportunities, influence opinions, and expose us to manipulation or judgment. But they're not permanent. With awareness and action, anyone can start to reclaim their privacy.

Because in the end, digital freedom isn't about disappearing—it's about choosing what to leave behind.

Chapter 3: Password Protection Made Simple

Passwords are the front doors to your digital life—and for many people, those doors are left wide open. Despite countless warnings about cyber threats, the most commonly used passwords remain shockingly weak: "123456," "password," and "qwerty" are still among the top choices. Worse yet, most people reuse the same password across multiple sites, making it incredibly easy for hackers to gain access to not just one account—but dozens.

Understanding password protection is one of the simplest yet most powerful ways to safeguard your online privacy. A strong password doesn't just keep out nosy advertisers or script kiddies—it can stop identity theft, financial fraud, and serious reputational damage. The best part? Creating a bulletproof password system doesn't require any special skills or software—just the right mindset and a few essential habits.

Let's start with the basics: what makes a password strong?

A strong password is long, unique, and complex. Ideally, it's at least 12–16 characters and includes a mix of uppercase and lowercase letters, numbers, and symbols. But strength alone isn't enough. The real power lies in uniqueness. If you use the same strong password for multiple sites, a single data breach can still compromise everything. Each account should have its own separate, strong password—especially for high-value targets like email, banking, and cloud storage.

Unfortunately, remembering dozens (or hundreds) of unique, complex passwords is unrealistic for most people. That's where password managers come in. Tools like Bitwarden, 1Password, Dashlane, or LastPass securely store and auto-fill your passwords. They encrypt your vault so even the company itself can't see your data. With a password manager, you only need to remember one master password. The manager does the rest—generating, storing, and filling your login credentials whenever needed.

Many password managers also detect weak or reused passwords and prompt you to update them. They can also store notes, personal IDs, and two-factor authentication (2FA) tokens, making them a one-stop shop for your secure login life.

Speaking of 2FA, it's one of the most critical layers of protection you can add to any account. Two-factor authentication requires you to verify your identity in two ways—typically your password plus a code sent via text, app, or email. This second layer drastically reduces the chances of a hacker breaking in, even if they somehow guess or steal your password.

But not all 2FA methods are equally safe. Text message (SMS) codes are better than nothing, but they can be intercepted or redirected through SIM-swapping attacks. A more secure option is using an authenticator app like Google Authenticator, Microsoft Authenticator, or Authy. These apps generate time-sensitive codes that change every 30 seconds, and they work offline—making them immune to network-based attacks.

Some users even prefer hardware security keys like YubiKey or Titan, which physically connect to your computer or phone to verify your identity. These keys are virtually unhackable and ideal for protecting high-security accounts like online banking, crypto wallets, or email used for business or legal matters.

Another often overlooked risk is password recovery. Many people set weak or predictable recovery questions, like their mother's maiden name or the name of their first pet. Unfortunately, this information is often easy to find on social media or public records. If your recovery process is weak, it can undermine even the strongest password. Always make recovery questions obscure or use false but memorable answers—and store them securely.

Be mindful of phishing attacks as well. Hackers often attempt to trick users into giving up their passwords voluntarily by mimicking login pages from banks, streaming services, or major retailers. These fake sites look almost identical to the real ones. A single slip-up—typing in your password on the wrong site—can give an attacker full access to your account. Always check the website address (URL), look for HTTPS, and never click on suspicious email links.

Another bad habit is saving passwords in browsers like Chrome or Safari without encryption. While convenient, these built-in password savers aren't nearly as secure as dedicated password managers, and they may be vulnerable if your device is compromised. If you do use them, make sure your device has strong local encryption and that your browser sync is protected by two-factor authentication.

For the ultra-cautious or those dealing with sensitive data, you can go even further. Consider using disposable email addresses or aliases for account registration, so even if a site is breached, your main email identity remains safe. You can also audit your accounts regularly, delete old or unused logins, and perform password updates every 6–12 months on critical accounts.

Let's not forget mobile devices. Make sure your phone or tablet is locked with a passcode—not just facial recognition or a fingerprint. These biometric methods are convenient, but not foolproof. In certain legal situations or at border crossings, you can be compelled to use a fingerprint or face scan, but not a passcode. Use both together when possible.

Finally, avoid sharing your passwords over email or text. If you must share access, use encrypted services like ProtonMail or password-sharing features built into tools like 1Password. And never, ever write passwords on paper unless it's kept in a physically secure location.

Password protection doesn't have to be complicated. It just requires a few smart decisions and the willingness to change old habits. In the next chapter, we'll explore how to secure your physical devices—because even the best digital hygiene can be undone if your phone or laptop falls into the wrong hands.

Nina the freelancer

Nina had always considered herself tech-savvy. As a freelance copywriter, she worked online, managed dozens of client accounts, and used every productivity tool available. Her digital world was fast, organized, and automated. But when her PayPal account was drained in under three minutes, everything changed.

It happened on a quiet Thursday morning. Nina was working from a café, sipping coffee while responding to emails, when she got the first notification: a $497 payment to a name she didn't recognize. Then another. And another. She froze. Her PayPal balance had dropped to zero—and her linked bank account was now in the negative. Her heart raced. She tried to log in, but the password no longer worked.

Frantic, she called PayPal support. After what felt like hours of hold music, the agent confirmed what she feared: someone had accessed her account, changed her password, and initiated multiple transfers. The strange part? There were no signs of phishing. No suspicious emails. No fake login pages. Just a clean, direct breach.

It didn't take long to figure out the weak link. Nina had used the same password for her PayPal account as she did for several other websites. One of those sites had suffered a data breach six months earlier—a site she hadn't even used in years. The leaked login credentials, including her email and password, had been dumped on the dark web. From there, it was only a matter of time before someone tried those credentials on PayPal—and it worked.

Worse, she hadn't enabled two-factor authentication. Her entire financial gateway had been guarded by one recycled password.

After the bank resolved the fraud and reversed the charges, Nina made a vow: this would never happen again.

She started with a password audit. She listed all the websites she used regularly—banking, email, online stores, social media, subscription platforms, and client portals. Then she checked each one for reused or weak passwords. The list was longer than she thought. Almost 70% of her accounts used a variation of the same phrase: her childhood nickname and a few numbers. Sometimes she added an exclamation mark or changed the last digit. She thought it was clever. It wasn't.

Next, she signed up for a password manager—Bitwarden. It was free to start, easy to install, and immediately suggested stronger replacements for her weak credentials. It could generate 20-character passwords made of gibberish—safe, random, and impossible to guess. With the click of a button, she updated her logins and stored each one in her encrypted vault. She no longer needed to remember dozens of codes—just one master password.

But she didn't stop there.

She added two-factor authentication to every account that offered it—especially her banking, PayPal, Google account, and cloud storage. She used Google Authenticator, which created codes that changed every 30 seconds. It was intimidating at first, but after a few days, it felt like second nature. The peace of mind was worth it.

She also set reminders to change her master password every 6 months and configured biometric lock on her phone's password manager. To take it further, she bought a YubiKey—a small USB device that required her physical touch to unlock high-security accounts. "If I lose my computer or phone," she thought, "they still won't get in."

Nina even changed the way she answered password recovery questions. Instead of real answers—like her first pet's name—she used random phrases only she would remember. She stored those in her notes inside the password manager, encrypted and protected.

A few weeks later, she was helping a fellow freelancer whose Instagram account had been hacked. "Do you use the same password for multiple things?" Nina asked. Her friend nodded. "You're not alone," she said. "But let me show you something that could save your life."

It wasn't just about security anymore—it was about awareness. Password protection wasn't some techy paranoia. It was the foundation of her digital independence. Nina realized that every time she locked her front door at night, she was protecting her physical life. And every time she updated a password, she was protecting her digital one.

A few months later, she gave a presentation to a local business group titled "Digital Locksmithing for Entrepreneurs." She showed them how to secure their accounts, use password managers, and stay ahead of data breaches. "This is the easiest cybersecurity upgrade you'll ever make," she said. "And the most important."

Looking back, she saw the breach not as a failure—but as a turning point. It was the wake-up call she never asked for but desperately needed. Today, her systems are airtight, her confidence unshakable. And every time she helps someone lock their digital doors, she's reminded that the most powerful tool online isn't an app or a firewall—it's good habits.

Chapter 4: Protecting Your Personal Devices

Your devices—smartphones, laptops, tablets, and even smartwatches—are portals into your digital life. They hold your personal photos, banking information, messages, emails, social media logins, and access to work files. In many ways, losing control of your device is like losing control of your identity. And yet, many people use these powerful tools without any real protection.

Securing your personal devices is one of the most important steps you can take toward protecting your online privacy. This chapter focuses on practical strategies to make your physical and digital devices more secure against theft, hacking, spying, and data loss. Whether you're using iOS, Android, Windows, or macOS, the principles remain largely the same—layered security, encrypted data, and controlled access.

Let's begin with **physical security**. The most basic and often overlooked step is enabling a lock screen with a passcode. Whether it's a PIN, password, fingerprint, or facial recognition, make sure your devices can't be accessed by just anyone. Avoid short PINs like "1234" or "0000." If you use a pattern lock, don't choose obvious shapes like a straight line or a letter. For best results, use biometrics *and* a strong backup passcode.

Always enable **automatic lockout timers**. If you step away from your phone or computer, it should automatically lock after 30 seconds to 2 minutes. This protects your data from curious strangers or opportunistic thieves in public places. On laptops, use screensavers that require a password to resume.

Next, consider **device encryption**. Most modern devices now come with encryption enabled by default. Encryption protects the data on your device so that even if someone steals it, they can't access the contents without your password. On iPhones, encryption is automatic once you set a passcode. On Android, it's usually under "Security > Encryption & Credentials." For laptops, look for FileVault (macOS) or BitLocker (Windows Pro) and turn it on if it's not already active.

Regular **software updates** are also a critical security measure. Operating system updates and app patches often include fixes for vulnerabilities that could be exploited by hackers. Set your devices to update automatically and check manually at least once a month. Outdated software is like a rotting fence—attractive to intruders and ineffective at keeping them out.

Use **trusted antivirus and anti-malware tools**, especially on Windows devices. While macOS and iOS have built-in protections, it's still wise to use additional layers. Malwarebytes, Bitdefender, Norton, and Avast are popular choices. They can detect spyware, trojans, and other malicious software that may hide on your device.

Avoid downloading apps or software from unofficial sources. Stick to the App Store, Google Play, or verified developer websites. Sideloaded apps or pirated software often come bundled with spyware or backdoors. If you root or jailbreak your phone, understand that doing so bypasses key security protections and increases your risk of exposure.

Be wary of **Wi-Fi and Bluetooth vulnerabilities**. Never connect to unsecured public Wi-Fi without using a VPN. Hackers can easily intercept your data using tools like packet sniffers, especially on networks with no password. Disable "auto-connect" to open networks and turn off Wi-Fi and Bluetooth when not in use. This not only protects your privacy but also improves battery life.

Bluetooth attacks, such as Bluejacking or Bluesnarfing, allow nearby attackers to send messages to your device or access data without permission. These attacks are rare but still possible. If you don't need Bluetooth, turn it off—especially in public.

Browser security on your device matters just as much as on desktops. Install privacy-respecting browsers like Brave or Firefox, and avoid using default browsers like Chrome without adjusting settings. Clear your browsing history, block third-party cookies, and use extensions like HTTPS Everywhere, uBlock Origin, and Privacy Badger to limit tracking and data leakage.

Control your device's **app permissions** aggressively. On most phones, apps request access to features like your camera, microphone, location, contacts, and storage. Many users simply tap "Allow" without realizing what they're giving up. Go to your phone's settings and review which apps have access to what. Deny access to anything unnecessary. A photo editing app doesn't need your microphone. A calculator shouldn't need access to your contacts.

Smart speakers, smart TVs, and voice assistants are growing privacy threats. Devices like Amazon Alexa, Google Nest, and Apple Siri are always listening for their trigger word. While they claim not to record anything until activated, researchers have shown that accidental triggers do happen. Check your voice assistant's settings to review or delete stored voice data. Mute the microphone when not in use, or place these devices in non-sensitive areas of your home.

Use **remote wipe and location tracking** features. If your phone or laptop is lost or stolen, tools like Find My iPhone (iOS), Find My Device (Android), or Find My Mac can help you locate or remotely erase the device. Make sure these are turned on and linked to your account. Losing a device is bad—but losing your personal data is worse.

Another often overlooked layer is **backup and recovery**. Privacy isn't just about keeping data away from others—it's also about not losing it yourself. Use encrypted cloud backups or physical encrypted hard drives to store your most critical files. Services like iCloud, Google One, Sync.com, or Tresorit offer varying degrees of privacy, depending on your encryption preferences. Just make sure your backups are also protected with strong passwords and 2FA.

Finally, consider the **social side of device security**. Avoid letting others use your devices unsupervised. Even friends or family may unintentionally open phishing links or download malicious files. Don't leave your devices unattended in public, even for a moment. Train yourself to treat your phone or laptop like your wallet—close to you, guarded, and locked down when not in use.

Your personal devices are the front lines of your digital identity. They are your tools, your memory, your communication lifeline—and often your only connection to the online world. Securing them is not optional. It's essential.

In the next chapter, we'll take a closer look at social media—where privacy often disappears without you even realizing it.

Now lets talk about Darren's story

When Darren's laptop disappeared from his backpack at a busy New York coffee shop, he told himself it was just a theft. Annoying? Yes. Inconvenient? Sure. But not devastating. After all, he had insurance and a backup at home. Or so he thought.

It wasn't until three days later that he realized what had really been taken.

The thief hadn't just stolen a device—they'd stolen access to his entire life. Darren hadn't enabled a lock screen password. His emails, cloud storage, and social media accounts were all signed in. He hadn't logged out in months. Whoever had the laptop had a front-row seat to his bank statements, contracts, client notes, and even private photos.

At first, nothing happened. But on the fifth day, he got an email from his business account: "Password successfully changed." A few minutes later, his clients received strange invoices. Then, his Instagram started posting spammy ads about cryptocurrency giveaways. He couldn't log in to stop it. His email, PayPal, and even his Dropbox had all been hijacked.

What hurt most wasn't the embarrassment—it was the loss of trust. One of his long-time clients emailed, "Is this a joke or did someone actually hack you?" Darren felt exposed and unprofessional. It had never occurred to him that someone stealing a device could turn into a digital disaster.

The next few weeks were a whirlwind of damage control. He filed a police report, froze his bank accounts, contacted tech support for every platform he could remember using. He went through multiple identity verification processes—some easy, some grueling. Many accounts were never recovered. But others were, thanks to a single saving grace: he had enabled two-factor authentication (2FA) on his primary Gmail account months earlier.

That 2FA wall stopped the attacker from reaching everything. But it was too late to undo all the harm.

When the dust settled, Darren made a new vow—he would never again treat device security as an afterthought.

He started with a new MacBook and a clean slate. First, he activated FileVault, Apple's built-in disk encryption. Now, if the device was stolen again, the data would be unreadable without his login. He enabled a 12-character alphanumeric password, not just a fingerprint. He also set the laptop to lock after 60 seconds of inactivity and made sure the screensaver required a password to resume.

Next, he turned on remote access with Apple's "Find My" feature. If the laptop went missing, he could locate it on a map—or erase it entirely. He tested it just to be sure. It worked.

He moved on to his phone. Darren had never thought much about app permissions before. But now he went app by app, revoking microphone, camera, and location access for anything that didn't need it. The flashlight app didn't need his GPS. A photo filter app didn't need access to his contacts. Most didn't need anything. He deleted over 20 apps in one night.

Then came the antivirus software. He installed Malwarebytes for his Mac and Bitdefender on his phone. They ran silent scans in the background but gave him a comforting sense of control. He also installed a VPN for when he worked at coffee shops, hotels, or airports. Now, every public Wi-Fi session was encrypted.

He switched from Chrome to Brave and Firefox and began using privacy extensions. Tracking ads stopped following him across the web. His online experience felt lighter—less invasive.

As for smart devices, Darren had always loved convenience. But he'd never reviewed the settings on his Alexa. It had recordings of his voice—entire conversations, even jokes he'd told friends. It felt unsettling. He deleted them all and muted the mic. "I can turn it on when I need it," he thought. "But I don't need it listening all the time."

Finally, Darren made it a routine: once a month, he checked device updates, app permissions, and did a quick privacy audit. He also set automatic cloud backups for key files using an encrypted backup service. "Losing data is bad," he said to a friend, "but losing control of it? That's worse."

Weeks later, another freelancer in his circle had a close call—her phone was stolen in a Lyft, and she hadn't set up a passcode. Darren helped her navigate recovery. "You'd be surprised how much is at risk when your screen isn't locked," he said. "It's like leaving your house with the door wide open."

Looking back, he realized that his previous approach—convenience over caution—had nearly cost him his business. Today, his mindset had shifted. Device protection wasn't about being paranoid. It was about being prepared.

His new motto? "It's not just a laptop. It's my life in aluminum."

Chapter 5: How to Stay Private on Social Media

Social media is one of the greatest threats to your online privacy—and ironically, it's also where people tend to share the most. Platforms like Facebook, Instagram, TikTok, X (formerly Twitter), LinkedIn, and Snapchat are designed to encourage engagement by tracking every click, scroll, and comment. What you post, what you like, who you follow, how long you hover on a video, even what you type and delete—all of it contributes to your digital identity.

The trade-off between connection and privacy is subtle but significant. On the surface, you're sharing moments with friends. Behind the scenes, you're giving platforms and advertisers a detailed behavioral map of your habits, interests, routines, personality, relationships, and even mental health.

Understanding how to manage your privacy on social media isn't about deleting everything. It's about taking control. With the right settings, behaviors, and boundaries, you can enjoy the benefits of social media while minimizing the risks.

Start with **your profile visibility**. Every social platform offers some form of privacy settings that control who can see your posts, photos, personal details, and friend list. Review them. On Facebook, for example, set your profile so only friends can see your posts—not the public or "friends of friends." On Instagram and TikTok, consider switching to a private account if you're not a public figure or business. On LinkedIn, limit profile visibility to only people you're connected with—or customize what the public sees.

Avoid sharing personal details in your bio or public posts. Information like your full birthdate, phone number, home address, school name, or workplace makes it easy for identity thieves to piece together your life. Even seemingly harmless details, like your pet's name or favorite band, can be used to guess password reset questions.

Next, examine **location sharing**. Many apps tag your posts with your location automatically. If you regularly post in real time from your home, gym, or child's school, you're essentially giving strangers a map to your daily life. Turn off geotagging in your camera and social media apps unless you have a specific reason to use it. If you want to share travel photos, wait until you've returned before posting. Real-time location data is one of the biggest security vulnerabilities for individuals and families.

Be cautious with **tagging and facial recognition**. Platforms like Facebook and Instagram can recognize faces and automatically tag you in photos—even if you didn't upload them. This creates an unofficial image library of your face across the internet. Go into your settings and disable automatic tagging or facial recognition features. Also, review and approve tags before they appear publicly on your profile. This not only protects your privacy but also your reputation.

Then, look at **third-party app connections**. You've probably used your social media login to sign into apps or websites. While convenient, these third-party connections often come with full access to your profile data—and sometimes your friends' data too. Go into your settings and revoke access to apps you no longer use. It's safer to use email or create separate logins for different services.

Audit your **post history**. Scroll through your old posts and consider what someone could learn about you. Do you talk about your routines, family, political opinions, or finances? Could a stranger use this information to impersonate you? Some platforms allow you to bulk delete or archive old content. Use this to your advantage. You can even download a copy of your data to see what the platform knows about you—it's usually more than you'd expect.

Now let's talk about **direct messages**. Many people assume that DMs are private, but most platforms have access to message metadata—and sometimes the content itself. Messaging apps owned by Meta (Facebook Messenger, Instagram DMs, WhatsApp) may scan messages for "security purposes" or use metadata to target ads. For truly private conversations, consider switching to end-to-end encrypted platforms like Signal, Telegram (secret chats only), or ProtonMail for email.

Avoid clicking on links or attachments from unknown sources, even if they appear to be from a friend. Social media is a hotbed for phishing scams, where attackers hijack an account and send malicious links disguised as funny videos, giveaways, or shocking news.

Limit **photo and video uploads** to what's necessary. Every image carries metadata (EXIF data) such as location, time, and device information. While some platforms strip this data on upload, others do not. Before posting, consider removing this metadata manually or using apps that sanitize images.

Pay close attention to **ad preferences and tracking**. Most social platforms allow you to see how they categorize you for advertisers. You can access your ad settings to turn off interest-based ads, remove categories, and prevent them from using your activity on other websites. While this doesn't stop all tracking, it significantly reduces the personalization—and exploitation—of your data.

Remember that **friends can compromise your privacy** too. If a friend tags you in a photo, shares your personal story, or posts something with you in the background, that content can be shared, downloaded, or reposted indefinitely. Have conversations with people close to you about what you're comfortable sharing publicly.

For parents, be especially mindful of what's called **"sharenting"**—sharing photos and stories about your children online. While it may seem innocent, this creates a digital footprint for your kids before they've had a chance to define it themselves. Bad actors have been known to scrape children's photos for scams or abuse. Always ask yourself: would I want this online forever if I were them?

Finally, understand that **deleting your account doesn't erase your data**. Social media companies often retain your information for months or years. Before deleting, download your data and carefully review what is saved. Some platforms allow you to deactivate temporarily while preserving your content offline.

Social media doesn't have to be a privacy nightmare. But it does require discipline, awareness, and a proactive approach. The next time you post, pause and ask: "Would I share this if I knew who was watching?" If the answer is no, reconsider. If the answer is yes—at least you're making that choice consciously.

In the next chapter, we'll cover private browsing and search engines—your tools for navigating the web without constantly being watched.

Lena and social media

Lena loved social media. As a lifestyle blogger and aspiring influencer, it was her playground, her stage, and her income stream. She posted daily: smoothie recipes, gym selfies, travel reels, outfit-of-the-day pics. Her followers loved her transparency. "Thanks for always keeping it real!" they'd comment. "You're so relatable!" she even live-streamed parts of her day, answering questions while walking through the grocery store or picking up her kids from school.

She didn't see herself as careless—just authentic. But that authenticity came at a cost she never saw coming.

It began with strange messages. First, a few DMs from anonymous accounts asking about her kids' names. Then a comment appeared on her recent post: "Nice gym routine. I saw you in person last Tuesday—same pink hoodie, right?" She laughed it off at first. But then she got an email from someone claiming to be a fan. They mentioned her street. Then the coffee shop she went to every Monday.

That was the moment her smile cracked.

She started to feel watched.

It got worse. A man showed up at her gym and asked the front desk if Lena was there. He knew her name, where she trained, even the name of her trainer. Security escorted him out, but the chill in her spine didn't go away. That night, she scrolled through her profile. Location tags, check-ins, visible routines, tagged friends, birthday celebrations–it was all there, all public.

She had built a digital map of her life for anyone to follow.

The next morning, Lena sat down and did something she'd never done before–she opened the privacy settings on every one of her social platforms. She was shocked. Her Instagram was wide open. Anyone could see her posts, stories, and tagged content. Her Facebook listed her phone number, birthdate, even her hometown. On TikTok, her likes and saved videos were public. She had granted access to dozens of third-party apps over the years. Most of them she didn't even remember using.

She began deleting.

She made her Instagram account private, removed personal contact info, and started approving tags manually. She removed hundreds of followers she didn't recognize. She turned off location tagging on her photos, deleted check-ins, and archived posts that showed where her kids went to school. On Facebook, she stripped her profile down to basics—first name, work, and profile picture. Everything else was hidden.

Then she addressed her DMs. She stopped accepting message requests from strangers and switched to Signal for private conversations with friends and collaborators. She posted a video explaining her new boundaries. "I love sharing my life with you," she said, "but I've realized I also need to protect it."

Lena didn't stop posting. But she changed how she did it. She started using generic captions instead of detailed updates. She stopped tagging her real-time location and waited to post photos from trips until after she'd returned. She moved behind-the-scenes content to a private email list for loyal followers, where she could control who got access.

She also talked with her husband and kids about boundaries. No more posting each other without permission. No geotagged family photos. No details about their home. It felt restrictive at first—but eventually it felt like freedom.

A few months later, she shared her story at a local women's business event. "I used to think oversharing meant connection," she said. "But now I know real connection starts with safety. If you're not protecting your digital space, you're not protecting your life."

She received a standing ovation—and dozens of messages from people who had never thought twice about what they posted. One woman said, "I didn't realize I was giving away so much... thank you for showing me how to pull it back."

Lena kept growing her brand—but with a new sense of clarity. Social media was still part of her business, but it wasn't her diary anymore. She chose what to share, when to share it, and who could see it. It wasn't about being secretive—it was about being intentional.

Today, Lena still posts regularly. Her audience continues to grow. But her presence online is curated, secure, and rooted in self-respect. Her message is simple: You don't have to disappear to be safe. You just have to stop giving strangers a map to your life.

Chapter 6: Private Browsing and Search Engines

Every time you open a browser and search for something–whether it's a health question, a financial tool, or the best Thai restaurant in your neighborhood–you're leaving behind a trail. That trail includes your search terms, browsing history, location, device type, time spent on pages, and often much more. This data is collected, analyzed, and shared across countless networks. In most cases, the goal is advertising. But in others, it can be surveillance, manipulation, or even criminal exploitation.

Most people believe that using "incognito mode" or "private browsing" makes their activity invisible. That's a myth. Private browsing simply prevents your browser from saving history and cookies locally on your device. It does **not** hide your activity from websites, your internet service provider (ISP), your employer (if on a work device), or the government. For true privacy, you need to go deeper.

Let's begin with **private browsing modes**, since many people use them without fully understanding what they do. In Chrome, Firefox, Safari, and Edge, private browsing prevents stored cookies, cached data, and search history on the device. It's helpful when logging into multiple accounts or using a shared computer, but it doesn't prevent trackers, third-party scripts, or browser fingerprinting. Think of it as clearing your footprints from your own path—but not the surrounding environment.

If you want to reduce online tracking, consider using a **privacy-focused browser**. Brave, Firefox (with privacy settings enhanced), and Tor Browser are among the top choices.

- **Brave** blocks third-party ads and trackers by default, upgrades connections to HTTPS, and includes fingerprinting protection. It also features a private browsing mode with Tor (more on that below).

- **Firefox** can be customized with extensions and stricter tracking prevention settings. It's open-source, actively maintained, and doesn't share your data with advertisers.

- **Tor Browser** is the gold standard for anonymity. It routes your traffic through multiple volunteer-operated servers (nodes), encrypting it at every step. However, it's slower and may break some websites due to aggressive privacy blocking.

For average users, switching from Chrome to Brave or Firefox already provides a significant privacy boost without sacrificing usability.

Next, address **search engines**. Google dominates the search space but is notorious for data collection. Every search you make is logged and tied to your IP address, location, and user profile (if you're signed in). This data is used to personalize ads, build behavioral profiles, and influence what results you see.

Instead, switch to **privacy-respecting search engines**:

- **DuckDuckGo** does not track or store your search history. It serves ads based on keywords—not user profiles.

- **Startpage** pulls results from Google but removes all identifying information from your request. It acts as a privacy filter.

- **Brave Search** is a growing engine that offers independent indexing and no tracking.

- **Mojeek** is one of the few engines that builds its own index and doesn't rely on Google or Bing. It's entirely independent and private.

Changing your default search engine in your browser or on your device settings is a powerful step. It ensures that every search—on mobile or desktop—starts with privacy in mind.

Let's also talk about **browser extensions**. These small add-ons can dramatically increase your online privacy. Top recommendations include:

- **uBlock Origin** – Blocks ads and trackers efficiently.
- **Privacy Badger** – Developed by the EFF, it learns and blocks invisible trackers.
- **HTTPS Everywhere** – Forces encrypted connections whenever possible.
- **ClearURLs** – Automatically strips tracking codes from URLs.
- **Decentraleyes** – Provides local versions of common web libraries to reduce third-party requests.

These tools work behind the scenes to clean up the web and protect you from surveillance. Be selective, though. Too many extensions can slow down your browser or even introduce risks. Only install extensions from trusted developers.

Another layer of protection comes from **Virtual Private Networks (VPNs)**. A VPN routes your internet traffic through an encrypted tunnel, masking your IP address and hiding your activity from ISPs and public Wi-Fi snoopers. Good VPNs also prevent websites from learning your real location and make it harder to build a profile based on your browsing.

Reputable VPN providers include ProtonVPN, Mullvad, IVPN, and NordVPN. Avoid free VPNs unless you've verified that they don't log your data. Remember: if you're not paying for the product, you may *be* the product.

If you're extra cautious, consider combining a VPN with private browsing and a privacy-friendly browser. For instance, using Firefox with strict settings + Startpage + a VPN creates a strong privacy shield for everyday browsing.

One often overlooked trick is **browser isolation**. Use different browsers for different tasks. For example:

- Firefox for social media accounts
- Brave for general browsing
- Tor for research or sensitive topics
- A separate browser profile for work vs. personal activity

This compartmentalization limits how much any one platform can learn about you. Cookies, trackers, and history stay isolated.

Lastly, consider the risks of **browser fingerprinting**. Even if you block cookies and hide your IP, websites can still identify you based on device information like screen resolution, fonts installed, time zone, browser version, and more. The more unique your setup, the easier it is to fingerprint you.

To combat this, tools like **CanvasBlocker**, **Trace**, or the **Tor Browser** help randomize or block fingerprinting data. Brave also includes fingerprinting protection built in.

In summary, here's your privacy-enhanced web browsing checklist:

1. Switch to a privacy-focused browser (Brave, Firefox, Tor)
2. Use private search engines (DuckDuckGo, Startpage)
3. Add tracker-blocking extensions (uBlock Origin, Privacy Badger)
4. Use a VPN on all devices, especially public Wi-Fi
5. Disable location and camera access for your browser

6. Avoid logging into accounts when unnecessary

7. Use browser isolation for compartmentalized activity

8. Stay mindful of fingerprinting and metadata leaks

Privacy on the web isn't about hiding in fear—it's about choosing when and how to be seen. In the next chapter, we'll go even deeper into private communication: how to protect your messages, emails, and calls from prying eyes.

Eli's Chrome story

Eli was a quiet guy—an engineer who worked remotely, lived modestly, and kept mostly to himself. But online, he was curious. He read about everything: obscure political movements, climate research, alternative medicine, and crypto technology. He loved going down internet rabbit holes, chasing ideas late into the night.

One evening, after watching a documentary about surveillance capitalism, Eli got paranoid. He searched for "how Google tracks users," and that led to "browser fingerprinting," and then to "how to browse privately." The results were unsettling. His favorite browser—Chrome—was logging everything. His search history had years of questions, some personal, some strange, most forgotten. His Google account was synced across his phone, laptop, and even his smart TV. Every move he made online was part of a growing digital profile.

He'd never done anything wrong, but the idea that someone could pull up a full psychological map of his online behavior made his skin crawl. Ads had been following him for years, but now he realized why. He wasn't just a user—he was a data point.

The final straw came when he searched for medical symptoms. For weeks afterward, he saw ads for treatments and clinics he hadn't even clicked on. It felt like his private fears had been sold off to the highest bidder.

That night, Eli made a change.

He downloaded **Brave**—a browser he'd heard blocks trackers by default. Immediately, his web experience felt cleaner. Fewer ads. No weird videos autoplaying. The pages loaded faster. Next, he switched his default search engine to **DuckDuckGo**. No more search suggestions tied to his history. No personalization. Just raw results.

Then he opened his Chrome settings and looked at what was being saved. Browsing history from three years ago. Autofill data for credit cards and addresses. His entire download history. Dozens of cookies from websites he hadn't visited in ages. He wiped it all out. It felt like sweeping the floor of a house he didn't realize had been filling with clutter for years.

But Eli didn't stop there.

He installed **uBlock Origin**, **Privacy Badger**, and **HTTPS Everywhere**—extensions that gave him a sense of control. He set Firefox up as a secondary browser and started using it exclusively for anything tied to his identity—banking, taxes, and work-related logins. He kept Brave for general browsing and DuckDuckGo searches. For particularly sensitive research, he tried out **Tor Browser**. It was slow, but effective.

To cover his tracks even further, Eli subscribed to **Mullvad VPN**, which didn't require an email to sign up. Now, his IP address was masked no matter where he went. He even set his VPN to auto-start when his device powered on, just in case he forgot.

He learned about **browser fingerprinting**—how websites could identify users based on technical specs. He tested his setup on a site called "Am I Unique?" The results shocked him: his browser had a unique fingerprint. It didn't matter that he'd blocked cookies. He was still identifiable. That led him to explore **CanvasBlocker** and **Trace**, extensions that scrambled his fingerprint. He enabled them cautiously, tweaking settings one by one until he found a balance that let his favorite sites work while obscuring his identity.

At first, it felt like overkill. But then he noticed something: he was no longer seeing eerily accurate ads. YouTube didn't feel like it was reading his mind. Search results were neutral again. He wasn't being nudged, steered, or profiled. He had become invisible—not because he was hiding, but because he'd taken back control.

One weekend, a friend visited and asked to borrow his laptop. The friend opened Google and started typing, but there were no suggestions, no pre-filled logins, no saved sites. "Dude, your internet's like a ghost town," he laughed.

Eli smiled. "That's the idea."

Months later, he gave a talk at a local library about digital privacy. The room was full of people who'd never thought twice about their browser. Eli showed them a live demo—two side-by-side browsers, one with default settings, the other locked down. The difference in trackers, pop-ups, and ads was staggering.

"You don't have to go off-grid," he said. "You just have to stop giving away your front door key."

People asked what the hardest part was. He thought for a moment and said, “Letting go of convenience. But once I did, I realized how much better the internet feels when it’s not watching you.”

Today, Eli still browses, searches, and explores—but on his own terms. He knows that privacy isn’t about paranoia. It’s about peace of mind. It’s about having the freedom to explore ideas without being turned into a product. And for him, that’s worth every extra click.

Chapter 7: Messaging, Email, and Secure Communication

Private communication is one of the most critical—and often most overlooked—aspects of online privacy. While most people assume their text messages, emails, and calls are secure, the reality is that many popular platforms are not built with privacy in mind. If you're using mainstream services like standard SMS, Gmail, or Facebook Messenger, your conversations are likely being scanned, stored, or even sold.

Whether you're discussing financial matters, health issues, business strategies, or just talking to loved ones, you have a right to confidentiality. Protecting your communication doesn't require becoming a cybersecurity expert—it just requires switching to platforms that prioritize encryption, transparency, and user control.

Let's start with **messaging apps**. Traditional SMS (text messages) is one of the least secure ways to communicate. Texts are not encrypted end-to-end, meaning your phone carrier—and potentially hackers or law enforcement—can access the content of your messages. Even iMessage, while encrypted between Apple devices, has vulnerabilities if backups are stored on iCloud without encryption.

For truly secure communication, use **end-to-end encrypted messaging apps**. The best options include:

- **Signal** – Open-source, free, and widely trusted. Signal offers full end-to-end encryption for text, voice, video, and group chats. It stores minimal metadata and does not log message content.

- **Telegram (Secret Chats only)** – Telegram's standard chats are cloud-based and not end-to-end encrypted. However, its "Secret Chat" mode is encrypted and offers features like self-destructing messages.

- **WhatsApp** – Provides end-to-end encryption by default, but because it is owned by Meta (formerly Facebook), it shares some metadata with the parent company.

- **Threema** – A paid app focused on privacy, with anonymous use and servers based in Switzerland.

Among these, **Signal** is widely regarded as the gold standard due to its transparency and commitment to privacy. It also allows users to set disappearing messages, biometric locks, and encrypted backups.

Next, let's discuss **email privacy**. Standard email providers like Gmail, Yahoo, and Outlook are convenient—but they scan your emails for data. Even if the provider doesn't read your content directly, it may scan attachments, log metadata, or index information to fuel advertising algorithms.

To move toward secure email, switch to **encrypted email services** such as:

- **ProtonMail** – Based in Switzerland, it offers end-to-end encrypted email, no IP logging, and anonymous sign-up. Proton also provides a secure calendar and file storage.
- **Tutanota** – Offers encrypted email, contacts, and calendars with strong privacy policies and no ads.
- **Mailfence** – A secure suite with encryption, calendars, and digital signing, ideal for business users.

Most secure email providers use **PGP (Pretty Good Privacy)** encryption or their own proprietary standards to ensure that only the sender and receiver can read a message—even the provider can't access the content.

You can further enhance email privacy by:

- Using **aliases** to hide your real address (via services like SimpleLogin or AnonAddy)
- Avoiding email on public Wi-Fi unless using a VPN
- Setting up **two-factor authentication (2FA)** for your inbox
- Avoiding email for sensitive information if more secure platforms (like Signal) are available

For high-risk users—activists, journalists, or people working with confidential data—consider combining encrypted email with a **custom domain** and your own mail server. This adds control, though it requires more technical knowledge.

Let's move to **voice and video calls**. Most people assume their calls are private, but standard phone calls can be tapped. Apps like Zoom, Skype, or FaceTime have varying degrees of security, but none are fully encrypted end-to-end in all situations.

Instead, use apps like **Signal** or **Jitsi Meet** for encrypted video and voice calls. Signal's calls are private by default. Jitsi is open-source and allows encrypted video conferencing with no sign-up required.

Now let's talk about **metadata**. Even if your message is

encrypted, metadata—such as who you contacted, when, and for how long—is often still collected. This data can reveal a great deal about your habits, location, and social network. Signal and ProtonMail minimize metadata collection, while most mainstream apps log it extensively.

To reduce metadata exposure:

- Use apps that minimize logging (Signal, Threema)
- Turn off read receipts and typing indicators
- Avoid linking your phone number if optional
- Use email aliases and non-identifiable usernames
- Avoid syncing contacts automatically

You should also take control over **message storage**. Many people don't realize that deleted messages may still be accessible in cloud backups, screenshots, or chat exports. To limit this:

- Set **disappearing messages** for personal chats (available on Signal, WhatsApp, and Telegram)
- Disable cloud backups, or use encrypted storage
- Regularly delete chat histories manually

- Educate your contacts on secure communication as well

Be cautious about **group chats**, which are harder to secure. If one member has poor device hygiene or saves transcripts, the entire chat may be compromised. Keep sensitive discussions in smaller, trusted groups using encrypted apps only.

And don't forget about **email trackers**. Many newsletters and marketing emails include invisible tracking pixels that report when you open them, what device you use, and where you are. To block trackers:

- Use **browser extensions** like Trocker or uBlock Origin
- Disable automatic image loading in your email client
- Open marketing emails in plain text when possible

In summary, here's your secure communication checklist:

1. Use Signal for text, voice, and video with trusted contacts
2. Use ProtonMail or Tutanota for email—especially for sensitive content
3. Avoid standard SMS or Gmail for private or legal matters

4. Enable disappearing messages, screen locks, and 2FA
5. Turn off metadata features like read receipts and contact syncing
6. Avoid public Wi-Fi without a VPN
7. Minimize storage and backup of sensitive communications

Privacy in communication isn't just about avoiding eavesdropping—it's about reclaiming intimacy, trust, and autonomy in a world that profits from your conversations.

In the next chapter, we'll shift focus to protecting your **identity and finances** from online scams, data breaches, and theft.

Amira's 2FA story

Amira was a freelance consultant working with clients all over the world. She had built her business from the ground up using Zoom, Gmail, Google Docs, and WhatsApp. Communication was everything. She was always reachable—texting with clients late at night, emailing across time zones, jumping from one platform to another. It was efficient, fast... and vulnerable.

She didn't think much about privacy until one day she received a strange email from a client in the UK: "Hey, just confirming—did you send this contract again? Something seems off." Attached was a copy of a proposal she had sent weeks earlier. But it wasn't quite the same. There were subtle changes. Her signature looked odd. The payment details were altered. Someone had duplicated her message, edited it, and sent it using an email address that looked just like hers—except for one letter.

The scammer had been monitoring her conversations and injected themselves into the thread without her or the client noticing. Her stomach dropped. Had they been reading her emails? How long had this been happening?

She immediately checked her Gmail account. There it was—a forwarded copy of every email sent to an unknown address. Her inbox had been compromised. She hadn't turned on two-factor authentication. Her password was old and reused. She realized she had no idea how long someone had been spying.

Amira was furious—and ashamed.

She changed all her passwords and enabled 2FA on every account she could think of. But she knew it wasn't enough. Her trust had been broken. So she began rebuilding her digital communication with privacy at the center.

The first thing she did was sign up for **ProtonMail**. It felt strange moving away from Gmail—so much of her life was embedded there. But ProtonMail was clean, simple, and encrypted. She created a new email address for sensitive communication and sent her clients an announcement: "For your safety and mine, I'll be using encrypted email moving forward."

Next, she downloaded **Signal**. At first, she thought it was just another messaging app—but it quickly became her favorite. It was fast, clean, and everything was private by default. She started moving clients and collaborators over one by one. Some were hesitant at first, but when she explained what had happened, they understood. "We should've done this sooner," one of them said.

She also installed **Jitsi Meet** for her video calls. No downloads, no tracking, and no registration. It wasn't as fancy as Zoom, but it worked—and it respected her privacy. For larger projects, she still used mainstream tools but was far more careful. She added passwords to meetings, used waiting rooms, and never reused links.

To protect against future email impersonation, she bought a custom domain and secured it with strong DNS and SPF records—steps she learned from a cybersecurity forum. It made her look more professional, and it gave her control. No more relying on third-party services that sold her data behind the scenes.

She also trained herself to watch for **phishing attempts**—those sneaky emails that looked real but weren't. She no longer clicked on links in emails. She verified payment details by phone. She turned off image loading in her inbox to stop email trackers. She even added an email alias for online subscriptions, separating her professional world from the marketing noise.

One night, she sat at her desk, looking at her dashboard. Signal. ProtonMail. Jitsi. SimpleLogin. Everything streamlined. No ads. No trackers. No surprises. She felt like she'd finally cleaned up a digital mess that had been building for years.

Her mindset had changed. She no longer thought of privacy as optional. It was part of her professionalism—part of her integrity. Just like wearing a seatbelt, it wasn't about fear. It was about responsibility.

Amira didn't keep her transformation to herself. She gave a presentation at an online freelancer summit called "How to Talk Without Being Tracked." Hundreds attended. She showed them how to set up encrypted email, use Signal, and protect their inboxes from spam and spoofing. The questions poured in. One attendee wrote: "I didn't even know I was exposed until now. Thank you."

Looking back, the attack had been a turning point. It wasn't just about stopping a scam. It was about redefining her boundaries. Today, Amira works with more clients than ever—but on her terms. Her communication is intentional, encrypted, and secure.

Because now, when she hits "send," she knows exactly who's receiving it—and who's not.

Chapter 8: Identity Theft and Financial Privacy

Your identity is one of your most valuable assets—and in the digital age, it's also one of the most vulnerable. With just a few pieces of information—your name, date of birth, address, and Social Security number—a cybercriminal can apply for loans, open credit cards, file fake tax returns, or drain your bank account. Identity theft affects millions of people each year and often goes unnoticed until major financial damage is done.

While complete protection from identity theft may not be possible, you can make yourself a far more difficult target. Securing your financial privacy requires a layered strategy that includes account safeguards, proactive monitoring, data minimization, and smart habits.

Let's begin with the fundamentals: **what is identity theft**? It occurs when someone uses your personal data without your permission, usually for financial gain. Common forms include:

- Opening credit accounts in your name
- Filing fraudulent tax returns to claim refunds
- Stealing medical benefits

- Applying for government assistance
- Using your information to commit crimes or evade law enforcement

Cybercriminals obtain this data in a variety of ways: phishing scams, data breaches, malware, stolen mail, or social engineering. But increasingly, identity theft starts with data that you unknowingly share online—through social media, online forms, or unsecured websites.

Start by **locking down your sensitive identifiers**. Your Social Security number (SSN), date of birth, and government ID should never be entered into unverified websites. Avoid emailing documents with personal identifiers—especially when applying for loans, jobs, or housing. Use secure file-sharing services or encrypted attachments instead.

Next, focus on **financial account security**. Every bank, credit card, and investment account should have the following in place:

1. **Strong, unique passwords**
2. **Two-factor authentication (2FA)**
3. **Alerts for logins, transactions, and password changes**

4. **Account recovery options updated regularly**

Be cautious when connecting to financial accounts through third-party apps or services. Always verify that they use bank-level encryption and offer a clear privacy policy. If in doubt, access your accounts through the institution's official website or app.

One of the most powerful tools in your arsenal is **credit monitoring and freezing**. In the United States, you're entitled to a free credit report each year from each of the three major bureaus—Equifax, Experian, and TransUnion—through AnnualCreditReport.com. Check these reports for unfamiliar accounts, inquiries, or errors.

For higher protection, consider placing a **credit freeze** on your file. A freeze restricts access to your credit report, making it difficult for fraudsters to open new accounts in your name. You can temporarily lift or "thaw" the freeze when you need to apply for legitimate credit.

If you're not ready for a freeze, set a **fraud alert** instead. This requires creditors to verify your identity before opening new accounts.

Be proactive with **identity monitoring tools**. Services like Aura, IdentityForce, or LifeLock offer monitoring for credit changes, dark web breaches, public records, and financial account activity. Some banks and credit cards now include free identity monitoring as part of their services.

Another overlooked risk comes from **public records and data brokers**. Companies like Spokeo, Whitepages, and PeopleFinder compile your information from public sources—voter registration, property records, court filings—and sell it. Fortunately, you can manually opt out of most of these databases. Websites like PrivacyDuck and DeleteMe offer paid services to handle opt-outs on your behalf.

Let's talk about **online shopping and payment privacy**. Avoid entering credit card information on unfamiliar or unsecured sites. Look for HTTPS in the URL and research the site's legitimacy before proceeding. When possible, use:

- **Virtual credit cards** – temporary, masked numbers that protect your real account info
- **Payment apps** with built-in fraud protection (Apple Pay, Google Pay, PayPal)
- **Prepaid debit cards** for lower-risk transactions

These tools reduce the chances of your real card number being exposed in a breach.

Be extremely careful with **phishing scams**. These may come via email, text, or even phone calls claiming to be from your bank, the IRS, or popular brands. Never click on suspicious links, and don't give out personal information unless you initiated the contact. Always navigate directly to a company's official website.

Consider creating **separate email addresses** for financial accounts versus general use. This can reduce exposure and make it easier to spot suspicious activity. Use aliases or email forwarding services (like SimpleLogin) to keep your real address private when signing up for new services.

If you use cloud storage (Google Drive, Dropbox, iCloud) for financial documents, secure it with 2FA, encryption, and limited sharing. Don't store unencrypted tax returns, ID scans, or account numbers on shared devices or folders.

And what if your identity *is* stolen?

Take immediate action:

1. **File a report** at IdentityTheft.gov (FTC)

2. **Contact affected institutions** to freeze or close accounts

3. **Place a fraud alert or credit freeze** with all three credit bureaus

4. **File a police report** if needed (especially if crimes are committed using your ID)

5. **Keep records** of all communications and recovery steps

The emotional toll of identity theft can be severe. Victims often report feelings of shame, anger, or helplessness. But staying informed and prepared reduces both your risk and your response time.

In summary, your financial and identity privacy strategy should include:

- Account-level security (passwords, 2FA, alerts)
- Credit monitoring and freezes
- Data broker opt-outs
- Secure online payment methods
- Phishing awareness
- Encrypted cloud storage for sensitive documents
- A personal response plan if something goes wrong

In the digital world, protecting your identity is protecting your freedom. It's not about living in fear—it's about living prepared.

Next, we'll shift gears and explore **online privacy for families and kids**, and how to create safe digital habits at home.

Now, lets go over a unique story

Thomas never expected his identity to be stolen—especially not before breakfast. It started with a text from his bank at 6:13 a.m. "Did you attempt a $4,200 wire transfer?" Half-asleep, he blinked at the message and froze. He hadn't. He opened his banking app and saw that the account was locked. The panic kicked in instantly. What was going on?

Over the next few hours, the nightmare unfolded. Someone had opened a credit card in his name. A loan application had been submitted under his Social Security number. Worse, they had already accessed his bank account using credentials stolen from a data breach at a retail store he hadn't shopped at in years. A criminal had pieced together enough of his personal information—from old accounts, social media, and online forms—to impersonate him.

Thomas felt violated. Not just financially, but personally.

Someone had stepped into his digital shoes and walked off with pieces of his life.

He had always thought of himself as a careful person. He didn't share too much online, didn't fall for spam emails. But now, with multiple calls to banks, credit bureaus, and the police behind him, he realized that caution wasn't the same as protection.

That evening, Thomas sat at his desk and started rebuilding his digital life—brick by brick.

First, he froze his credit with all three major bureaus: Experian, Equifax, and TransUnion. It only took about 20 minutes total, but it made a world of difference. No one, not even *he*, could open a new line of credit until he manually lifted the freeze. He also set fraud alerts to notify lenders that they should verify any future credit requests under his name.

Next, he created accounts on **AnnualCreditReport.com** and downloaded his reports. There were five unfamiliar inquiries listed—evidence of the fraud. He filed disputes with each bureau and sent supporting documents. Then he submitted a report through **IdentityTheft.gov**, which helped him generate letters for creditors and a recovery plan.

Thomas also reviewed every financial account he had. He changed passwords, enabled two-factor authentication, and removed old email addresses that were no longer secure. He signed up for account login alerts and transaction notifications so he would never be caught off guard again.

Then he took aim at the data brokers. One by one, he searched for his name on sites like Whitepages, Spokeo, and MyLife. To his surprise, most of them listed his full name, age, previous addresses, phone number, and even the names of relatives. Anyone could pay $5 and download his personal profile. He spent an entire weekend opting out of every site he could find. It felt tedious—but necessary. "I'd never leave my front door open," he thought. "Why should I leave my digital life exposed?"

He also started using a **password manager** and created unique logins for every account. No more reusing the same phrase with a number at the end. He switched to **virtual credit cards** for online purchases—temporary, masked numbers that linked to his real account but expired after a single use. He signed up for **ProtonMail** and moved all of his financial emails to a new, private address. It was like getting a new key for a house that had been broken into.

Later that month, Thomas attended a local cybersecurity

workshop. He wasn't alone. Dozens of others had similar stories—people who had clicked on the wrong email, used the same password too many times, or filled out one too many online forms without thinking twice. "The scariest part," he shared during a Q&A session, "was that I didn't even know I was vulnerable. I wasn't reckless—I just wasn't prepared."

Over time, Thomas became the privacy advocate in his circle. He taught his family how to freeze their credit. He showed his sister how to use anonymous email aliases for job applications. He even helped his parents clean up their online profiles and start using secure messaging apps.

Months later, he got a letter from one of the banks that had denied the fraudulent loan request. It read: "Application denied due to identity mismatch." He smiled. His defenses were finally working.

Thomas never forgot how it felt to be blindsided. But he also never forgot how empowering it felt to take control again.

For him, privacy wasn't about hiding. It was about standing tall. It was about securing the foundation of who he was—his name, his voice, his choices—before someone else tried to claim them.

Chapter 9: Online Privacy for Families and Kids

In the modern household, privacy isn't just an adult concern—it's a family affair. Children are growing up in a digital world where their habits, preferences, voices, images, and even biometric data are being collected from a young age. Whether it's through educational apps, smart toys, YouTube channels, or social media, kids are being tracked—often without understanding the risks or giving real consent.

As a parent or guardian, protecting your child's online privacy may feel like an overwhelming task. But with the right tools, awareness, and boundaries, you can create a digital environment that empowers your kids to explore safely while keeping their personal information out of the wrong hands.

Start by understanding the scope of **data collection in children's platforms**. Many apps and websites aimed at kids track behavior, usage patterns, and even keystrokes. Some gather location data, voice recordings, or access the camera. Although laws like **COPPA** (Children's Online Privacy Protection Act) in the U.S. restrict how companies can collect data from children under 13, enforcement is inconsistent—and many apps are designed to skirt these rules by targeting "families" rather than "kids."

That's why **parental oversight** is essential. The first step is to limit exposure. Children under a certain age should not have unfettered access to the internet. Use kid-specific operating systems (like Amazon FreeTime or iPad Kid Mode) and configure **family safety settings** on every device. Both iOS and Android offer parental controls that can restrict app downloads, block certain websites, manage screen time, and require approval for purchases or content access.

Next, review and manage **app permissions**. Many children's apps request unnecessary access to the camera, microphone, contacts, or location. These permissions can be revoked in device settings. Ask yourself: does a coloring app really need GPS? If the answer is no, deny the request or delete the app entirely.

It's also important to **talk openly with your children** about digital footprints. Even at a young age, kids can understand the basic concept of privacy. Teach them not to share their full name, address, school, or phone number online. Encourage them to come to you if they encounter strange behavior, pop-ups, or messages from strangers. Use role-playing to practice what to do in suspicious online situations.

Social media introduces another layer of complexity. Most platforms set a minimum age of 13, but many children join earlier. If your child is using platforms like TikTok, Instagram, or YouTube, help them:

- Set their profile to private
- Turn off location sharing
- Use a pseudonym or first name only
- Avoid posting personal identifiers
- Disable direct messages from strangers
- Limit who can see, comment, or tag them in posts

Better yet, delay social media use until they're mature enough to understand the long-term impact of sharing online. Every post can be copied, saved, and reshared—even if deleted. Help them grasp that the internet has a memory.

Parents must also consider **their own behavior online**, especially with "sharenting"—posting photos, videos, or stories about your kids on social media. While it may seem harmless, these posts often reveal names, birthdays, locations, routines, and even faces that can be scraped by facial recognition tools or repurposed by malicious actors. Before sharing, ask: would my child consent to this later? Will they be okay with this photo existing forever?

You can further protect your family by using **child-friendly search engines** like Kiddle or KidRex, and **safe educational platforms** that don't rely on advertising revenue. Choose learning tools and games that have clear privacy policies and do not sell or monetize user data. Support companies that offer data minimization and allow you to delete accounts and data easily.

Install **ad blockers and tracking protection** on all household devices. Kids should not be targeted with manipulative ads based on their browsing habits. Browsers like Brave or Firefox (with parental controls) are safer than default options like Chrome. You can also install tools like **CleanBrowsing** or **OpenDNS Family Shield** to filter inappropriate or unsafe content at the network level.

It's a good idea to **limit smart devices** like Alexa, Google Home, and internet-connected toys in children's bedrooms. These devices often listen continuously and can record or transmit data without full transparency. If you use them, disable recording logs and review privacy settings regularly.

Educate yourself on **phishing and scams targeting children**. Kids may not recognize fake giveaways, "free game downloads," or pop-ups that trick them into entering personal details. Browser extensions that block pop-ups and deceptive ads can help, but guidance and conversation are your strongest tools.

Create a **family digital privacy plan**, including rules like:

- No sharing of personal info online
- Always ask before downloading an app
- Talk to a parent before replying to messages from unknown users
- Use strong passwords and never share them with friends
- Log out of accounts on shared devices
- Use screen time as a cue for a privacy check-in

Finally, lead by example. If you expect your kids to value privacy, show them what that looks like. Let them see you adjusting your settings, questioning app permissions, or using encrypted tools. Make privacy part of normal conversation—not just a punishment or fear tactic.

In summary, keeping kids safe online isn't just about blocking websites—it's about building lifelong habits. Empower your children to be curious, creative, and connected—but with boundaries. The digital world is here to stay. Your role is to make sure they grow up in it with safety, self-awareness, and respect for their own information.

In the next and final instructional chapter, we'll tie everything together with a system for building lifelong digital privacy habits—for yourself and those you care about.

Sofia's future

Sofia always thought she was being a good mom. She took pride in her daughter Emma's creativity and confidence. When Emma started making funny videos on her tablet, Sofia encouraged her. At first, they were just silly skits and dance routines filmed in their living room. Sofia would post them on Facebook or Instagram with captions like "Future star right here! " Friends and family loved them. The likes and hearts poured in.

But then things started to shift.

Emma, now ten years old, started asking to post the videos herself. She wanted a TikTok account, like her classmates. She had heard that some kids "went viral" and got free stuff or even became famous. Sofia hesitated, but eventually gave in—under one condition: she would monitor everything.

At first, it seemed innocent. Emma danced, lip-synced, and made crafts. Her follower count climbed quickly. Then one day, Sofia glanced at the comments section of Emma's latest post. There were dozens—some from other kids, others clearly from adults pretending to be younger. One comment said, "You're really pretty. Want to chat?" Another asked where Emma lived. One account had no profile picture, no posts, and a username filled with numbers.

Sofia's stomach dropped.

She deleted the video, then the entire account. Emma cried for hours. "Why are you ruining everything?" she asked. Sofia didn't know how to explain that she had unknowingly opened a window into their lives—and strangers had looked in.

That night, Sofia stayed up late reading about online safety for kids. She discovered how apps collect data—even from children. She read about facial recognition scraping images, data brokers building profiles on minors, and predators using innocent videos to find vulnerable targets. She had thought being present was enough. It wasn't.

The next day, Sofia sat down with Emma and made a new plan.

They reset every device. On Emma's tablet, they turned off location sharing, camera access for non-essential apps, and disabled the microphone where possible. Sofia installed

Family Link and used it to set time limits, approve new apps, and filter content. They also switched Emma's browser to **Kiddle**, a kid-safe version of Google with filtered results and no ads.

Sofia created a new shared email address for Emma's online activities—one that didn't include her full name or personal details. They talked about usernames and why it's safer not to include birthdays, school names, or anything identifiable.

Then came the hard part—Sofia had to take responsibility for her own oversharing.

She scrolled back through her Instagram and Facebook accounts. Dozens of baby photos, first-day-of-school pictures, birthday parties, Emma in her soccer uniform—with her school name clearly visible. Unknowingly, she had given away more information than Emma ever had. Sofia began removing them. It hurt, a little. Those were memories. But they weren't hers alone to share anymore.

They also talked about digital consent. Emma learned that just because someone asks you something online doesn't mean you have to answer. That privacy means you don't have to perform for strangers. That she was allowed to say no—to comments, messages, and even adults. Sofia watched her daughter absorb these ideas, and for the first time, Emma didn't resist. She felt more in control.

As the weeks passed, their routine changed. They created a shared digital calendar, scheduled screen-free weekends, and started using **Signal** to chat with close friends and family. Emma still made videos—but now they were stored on a private folder, shared only with grandparents and a few trusted friends. Sofia and Emma made them together, and they laughed more, now that there was no pressure to "go viral."

At school, Emma began noticing things her friends didn't—how some apps asked for weird permissions, or how sponsored content tried to trick them. She became the privacy champion in her class. One day, she told her teacher, "Did you know that app sells your data?" Sofia smiled when she heard the story.

Later that year, they hosted a "Digital Safety Night" at the local library. Parents came. So did teachers and even a few teens. Sofia and Emma stood in front of the crowd, side by side, and shared their story—what they had learned, what had scared them, and what had changed.

Sofia ended the talk with one simple idea: "We don't want to raise our kids to be afraid of the internet. We want them to be aware. And we want to protect them—not just by saying no, but by saying yes to smarter habits."

The applause was loud, but what stuck with Sofia was a message she received the next day: "Thank you. I didn't realize I was giving away my child's story until you shared yours."

Sofia now believes that privacy is a gift we pass down. Not just through rules and restrictions, but through example, trust, and conversation. And in their home, digital safety is no longer a lecture—it's a lifestyle.

Chapter 10: Building Lifelong Privacy Habits

By now, you've explored the major areas of online privacy—from passwords and social media to secure messaging, device protection, and financial safety. But knowledge without consistent action fades. That's why this final chapter focuses on converting your awareness into lifelong privacy habits that evolve with you. In today's data-driven world, privacy is no longer a one-time fix—it's a daily practice.

Start by shifting your mindset. Privacy isn't about hiding—it's about **choosing what to share, with whom, and when**. It's about exercising your digital boundaries just like you do physical ones. You wouldn't let a stranger walk through your home without permission. You shouldn't let unknown companies or bad actors walk through your data either.

To maintain long-term digital privacy, create a system of **monthly, quarterly, and annual habits**. These small routines compound into powerful protection.

Monthly Privacy Habits

1. **Review Device Settings**: Go through your phone and computer's app permissions. Revoke access to your

camera, microphone, location, and contacts from any app that doesn't absolutely need it.

2. **Clear Your Browsing Data**: Delete cookies, cache, and browsing history on all devices. Use browser extensions to block trackers and strip tracking codes from URLs.

3. **Check for Software Updates**: Update your operating systems, apps, antivirus software, and firmware on smart home devices. Many updates include patches for recent vulnerabilities.

4. **Scan for Leaks or Breaches**: Use tools like HaveIBeenPwned or your password manager to check if your email or login credentials have been compromised.

5. **Enable Disappearing Messages**: On messaging apps like Signal or WhatsApp, review conversations and enable disappearing messages for non-essential chats.

6. **Monitor Account Activity**: Log in to key financial accounts, Google, Apple, and social media platforms to review login history and connected devices. Remove unknown logins immediately.

Quarterly Privacy Habits

1. **Audit Your Online Accounts**: Make a list of all active accounts and delete or deactivate the ones you no longer use. Less exposure = less risk.

2. **Update Passwords for High-Risk Accounts**: Change passwords for email, banking, and cloud storage. Use a password manager to generate and store them securely.

3. **Check Privacy Settings on Social Platforms**: Social media platforms often update their policies and settings. Revisit your account visibility, ad preferences, and tagging permissions.

4. **Run a Google Search on Yourself**: Search your name, usernames, and email addresses. Take note of what's visible publicly and take action to remove outdated or sensitive content.

5. **Test Your Browser Fingerprint**: Visit amiunique.org or coveryourtracks.eff.org to see how unique and trackable your device is. Adjust browser settings or use privacy tools accordingly.

6. **Review VPN and Privacy Tools**: Make sure your VPN is active and configured properly. Replace expired privacy tools or subscriptions as needed.

Annual Privacy Habits

1. **Download Your Data**: Platforms like Google, Facebook, Apple, and others let you download a copy of the data they've stored about you. Review it—it's often eye-opening.

2. **Freeze Your Credit (if not already done)**: A credit freeze remains one of the most effective ways to stop identity theft. It's free and can be easily lifted if you apply for new credit.

3. **Opt Out of Data Brokers**: Visit sites like Whitepages, Spokeo, PeopleFinder, and others to remove your information. Services like DeleteMe or PrivacyDuck can automate this.

4. **Create a Digital Emergency Plan**: List your key accounts, 2FA recovery methods, and passwords (securely stored in your password manager). Include instructions for a trusted person in case something happens to you.

5. **Review Smart Home and IoT Device Settings**: Devices like smart speakers, TVs, security cameras, and thermostats collect vast data. Disable unnecessary

features like always-on microphones or motion recording in private areas.

6. **Reflect on Digital Boundaries**: Ask yourself what has changed in the past year—new jobs, relationships, platforms, or habits? Update your privacy approach accordingly.

Long-Term Mental Habits

- **Think Before You Share**: Before you post, comment, or click "allow," ask: "Do I need to share this? Who benefits from this data?"

- **Default to Deny**: When apps ask for permissions, treat every request with skepticism. Only allow access when absolutely necessary.

- **Be Skeptical of "Free"**: If a service is free, it likely makes money by selling your data. Choose paid or open-source alternatives when possible.

- **Avoid Convenience Over Caution**: Saved passwords in browsers, autofill payment info, and open Wi-Fi are all conveniences that come with high privacy costs.

- **Stay Curious**: Privacy tools, scams, and threats evolve quickly. Stay informed through newsletters, podcasts, or YouTube channels that focus on digital safety.

Remember, privacy is not binary—it's a spectrum. You don't need to go full off-grid to reclaim control. Even implementing a few key habits will make you harder to track, less exploitable, and more in command of your digital life.

Above all, privacy is **a form of respect**—for yourself, your family, your boundaries, and your future. Make it part of your identity. Pass it on. And keep building a digital world where safety isn't a luxury—it's the default.

In the final story chapter, we'll explore what it looks like to live a privacy-first lifestyle, and how one family changed everything by making the shift together.

Marcus and Angela's password story

For years, Marcus and Angela had lived like most modern families—connected, convenient, and completely unaware of how exposed they really were. Between smart TVs, school tablets, online banking, and dozens of streaming subscriptions, their digital life was packed with logins, voice assistants, and autofill passwords. They weren't careless. They were just busy.

But everything changed after a family friend had her identity stolen. It was a wake-up call. That friend, a single mom, had spent six months untangling her accounts from fraudulent loans and social media impersonators. The emotional toll hit Angela hard. "That could be us," she told Marcus one night, sitting at the kitchen table after putting their kids to bed. "We share so much without thinking."

So they decided to make a change—not a one-time cleanup, but a permanent shift in how their family approached privacy.

They started small. Marcus bought a password manager. He spent an entire weekend replacing every reused password with long, random strings. Angela created a family privacy folder where they kept encrypted backups of critical documents and recovery codes. Together, they set calendar reminders: once a month, review permissions; once a quarter, check their credit reports; once a year, revisit social media settings.

They called it "The Digital Housekeeping Plan."

Their two kids, ages 9 and 13, were skeptical at first. No more random app downloads? No posting TikToks at school? But Marcus turned it into a game. "Privacy Points," he said. "Every smart move earns you points. The winner picks Friday movie night." The kids loved it. Soon, they were competing to see who could spot more tracking cookies or clean up the most app permissions.

Angela took it further. She opted out of every data broker she could find. It took time—but she found satisfaction in shrinking their family's digital footprint. She stopped using her real name in email addresses and unsubscribed from dozens of newsletters that tracked her clicks. She even deleted her Facebook account, realizing she hadn't truly enjoyed it in years.

They began treating online privacy like any other family value—something that had to be taught, talked about, and practiced regularly. At dinner, they shared "digital wins." At bedtime, they read stories—but also checked which apps the kids had used that day. When their son asked why they couldn't just "trust the apps," Marcus answered, "Because trust should be earned—and too many companies don't deserve it."

Their internet habits changed dramatically. They moved from Chrome to Brave. From Gmail to ProtonMail. From Alexa to manual light switches. They started using Signal instead of regular texting, and their smart TV was unplugged when not in use. They even stopped using their real birth dates and ZIP codes when filling out online forms—substituting anonymized data whenever possible.

One weekend, the kids helped build a "privacy fort"—a family-wide challenge to see how invisible they could become online. They mapped out every device, checked every permission, and deleted unused accounts. The youngest, who once complained about screen time limits, now boasted that his tablet had fewer trackers than his friends'. It became a badge of honor.

Six months in, something shifted. Life slowed down. Fewer notifications. Less noise. No more scam calls or creepy ads. They felt calmer, more focused. Angela said, "I didn't realize how much mental space was being eaten up by all the noise." Marcus agreed. Privacy didn't feel like fear anymore—it felt like freedom.

One evening, while helping their daughter with a school project about "values at home," she wrote, "My family values honesty, kindness, and privacy." Angela's eyes welled up. They had done more than install tools—they had created a culture.

The next week, Marcus was invited to give a talk at his company's "Digital Wellness Day." He shared their story—not as experts, but as a regular family that decided to take control. His final slide read: "Privacy isn't something you buy. It's something you build. One habit at a time."

Today, their routine continues. Monthly reviews. Quarterly resets. Yearly audits. It's just part of life—like brushing teeth or locking the front door. They still stream movies, use apps, and browse the web. But they do it intentionally, with awareness and agency.

And they sleep better for it.

The Power of Choice in a Watched World

We live in an age of unprecedented access. We can message friends across the world in seconds, learn anything with a single search, stream movies on demand, and automate our homes with a word. But with every new feature comes a new tradeoff. Convenience has crept into every corner of life—often at the cost of our personal privacy.

The truth is, most people never actively chose to give away their data. It just happened. A quick "Agree" to the terms. A saved password here, a synced calendar there. And before long, companies knew more about them than they knew about themselves.

But what if we could change that?

This book was never meant to scare you into disconnecting or make you feel ashamed of past habits. It was designed to empower. Because privacy isn't about paranoia—it's about power. It's about reclaiming your ability to move through the digital world on your own terms. It's about knowing the difference between being the product and being the customer. Between passive consumption and conscious choice.

What you've learned across these ten chapters isn't a

checklist—it's a mindset. You now know how to create strong passwords and why they matter. You understand that private browsing isn't truly private, and that encrypted messaging is no longer just for whistleblowers or coders—it's for everyone. You've seen how identity theft can devastate a life, how children are quietly tracked by seemingly harmless apps, and how social media, left unchecked, can turn your life into an open book written for someone else's profit.

But more importantly, you've seen how ordinary people—parents, freelancers, students, families—can turn things around. You've seen how taking control of your privacy is possible, realistic, and deeply rewarding. You've seen that it doesn't require you to vanish. It just requires you to *think* before you click. *Review* before you accept. *Ask* before you allow.

And perhaps that's the biggest shift of all: realizing that privacy is no longer something guaranteed. It's something you must *choose*—again and again.

This doesn't mean living in fear. It means embracing *awareness*. Just as you wouldn't leave your home unlocked or hand your wallet to a stranger, you shouldn't leave your data wide open to entities that haven't earned your trust. You have a right to boundaries—even in the digital world. Especially there.

Moving forward, your privacy practice won't be perfect. That's okay. There will be slip-ups. You'll forget to update a password, skip a setting, or download an app that knows more than it should. But the difference now is that you'll *notice.* You'll know how to respond. And you'll keep getting better.

Because privacy isn't a destination. It's a journey. A lifestyle. A form of digital self-respect.

So, what now?

Maybe you go review your passwords. Maybe you teach your child how to spot a scam. Maybe you finally download Signal, switch your search engine, or delete an account you've outgrown. Start anywhere. Start small. But start.

And when you do, you'll join a growing global movement—one where citizens, not corporations, decide the terms. One where technology serves people, not the other way around. One where you're not just a user—but a protector of your own digital space.

You don't need permission to protect your privacy. You just need the will.

Choose it. Practice it. Pass it on.

And never forget: in a world that profits from your exposure, your privacy is an act of resistance—and a declaration of freedom.

www.ingramcontent.com/pod-product-compliance
Lightning Source LLC
LaVergne TN
LVHW022009200926
848481LV00007B/2302